Brian Gagg

AF200460

THE CORONA COLORING AND PAINTING BOOK

Bibliografische Information der Deutschen Nationalbibliothek:

Die Deutsche Nationalbibliothek verzeichnet diese Publikation in der Deutschen Nationalbibliografie; detaillierte bibliografische

Daten sind im Internet über http://dnb.dnb.de abrufbar.

© 2020 Brian Gagg; 1. Auflage

Covergrafik, Texte & Illustrationen © 2020 Brian Gagg

Herstellung und Verlag: BoD – Books on Demand, Norderstedt

ISBN: 9783751902625

Content   Page

Viruses

Body defense cells

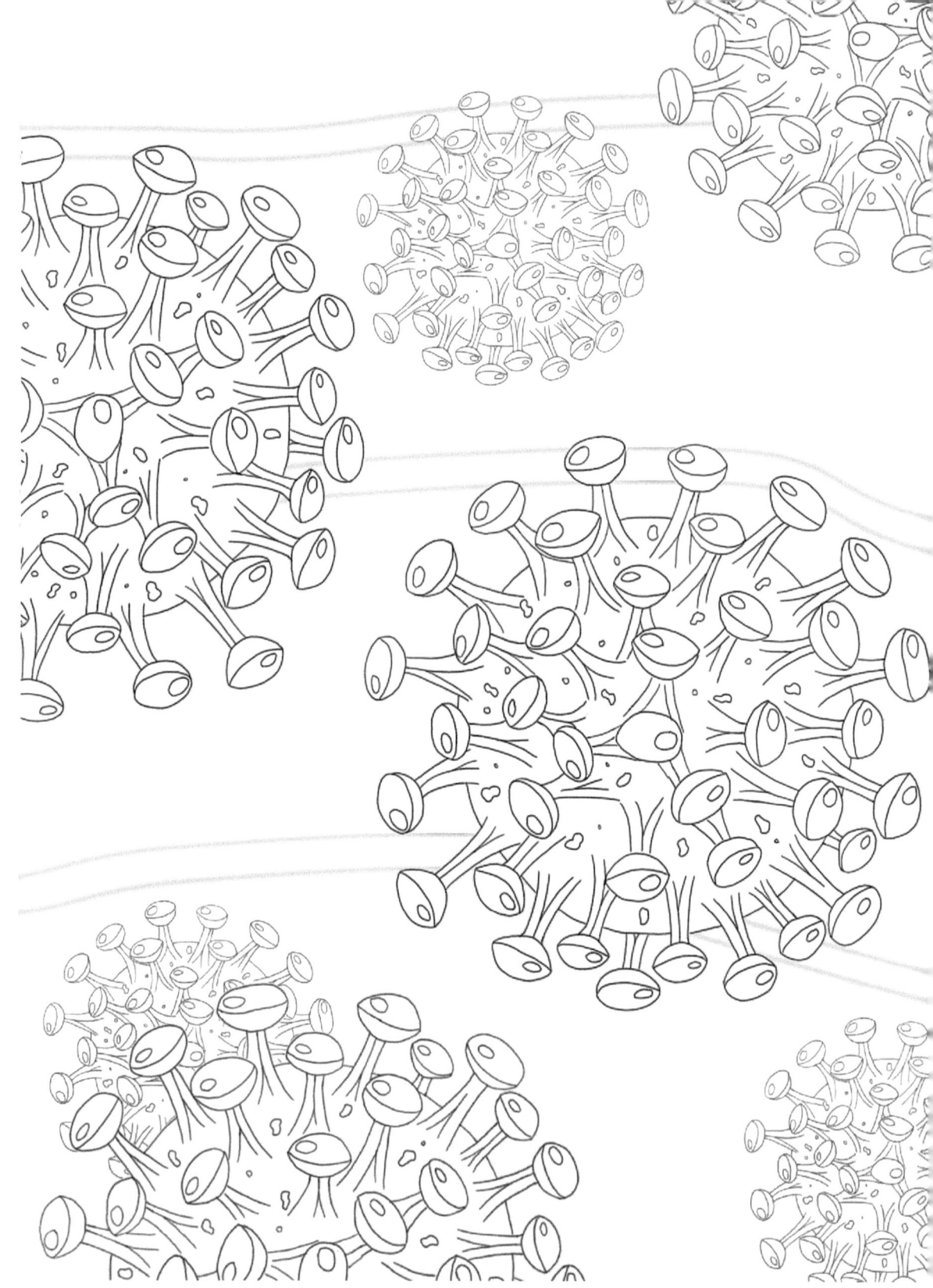

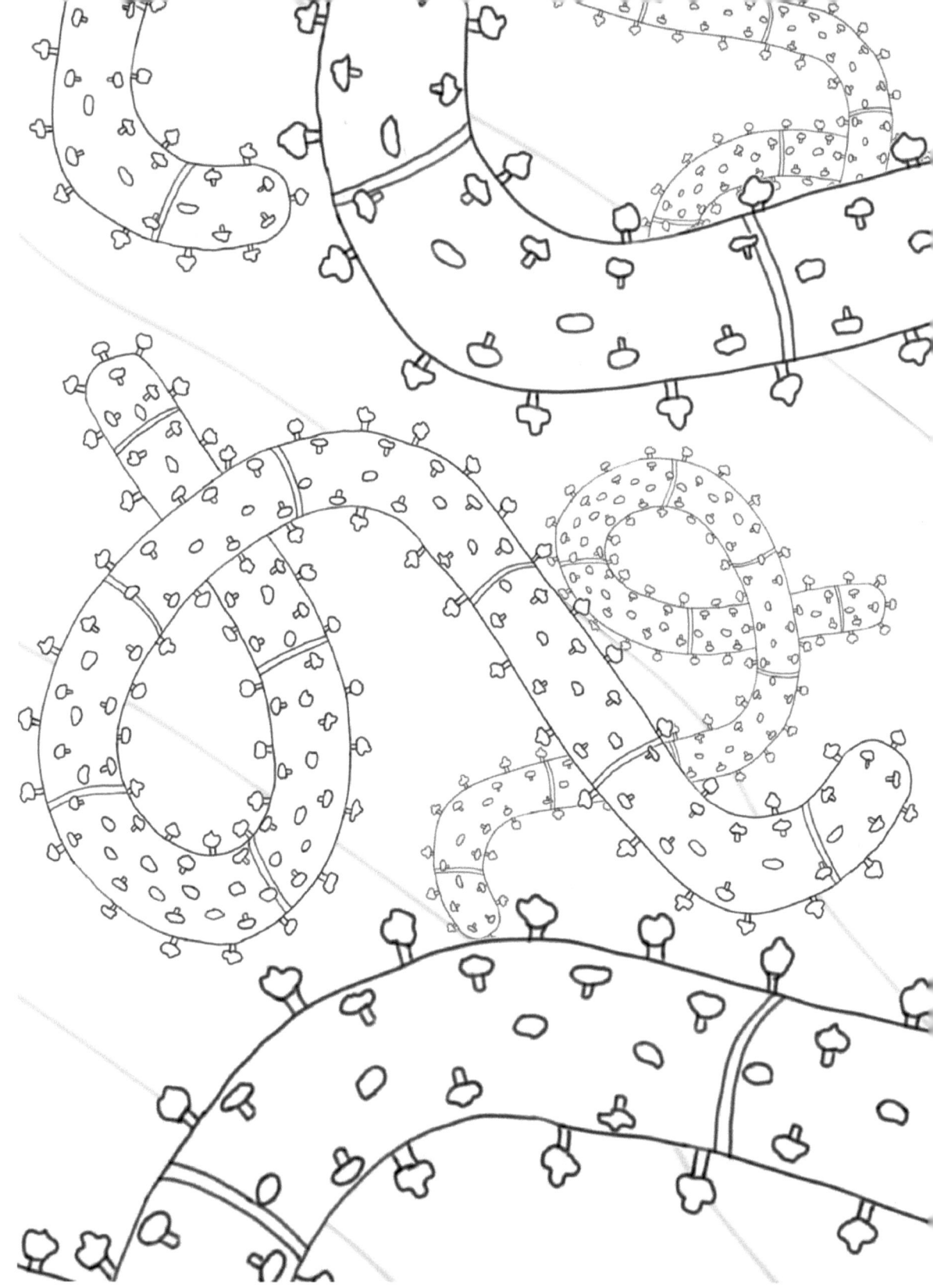

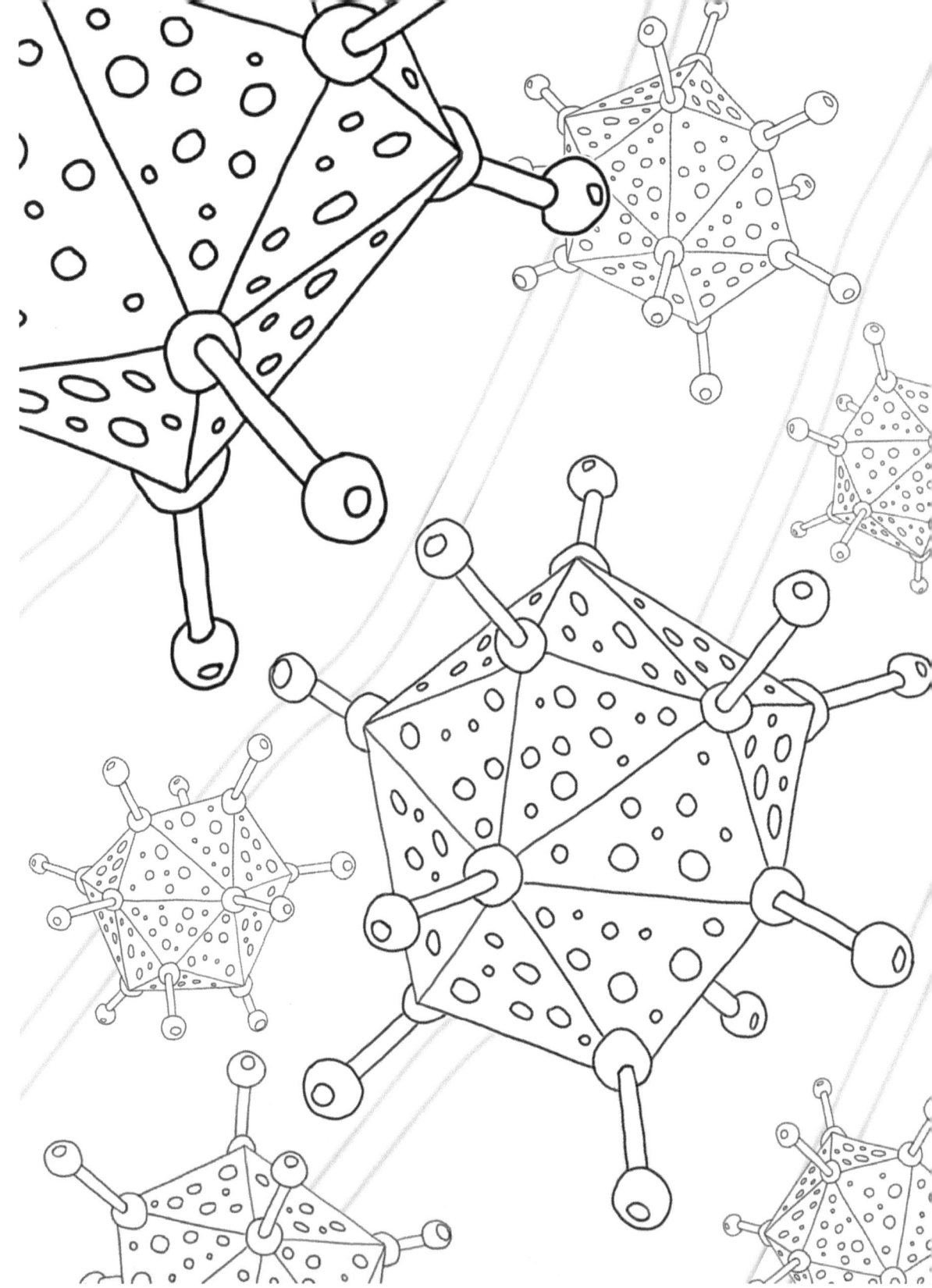

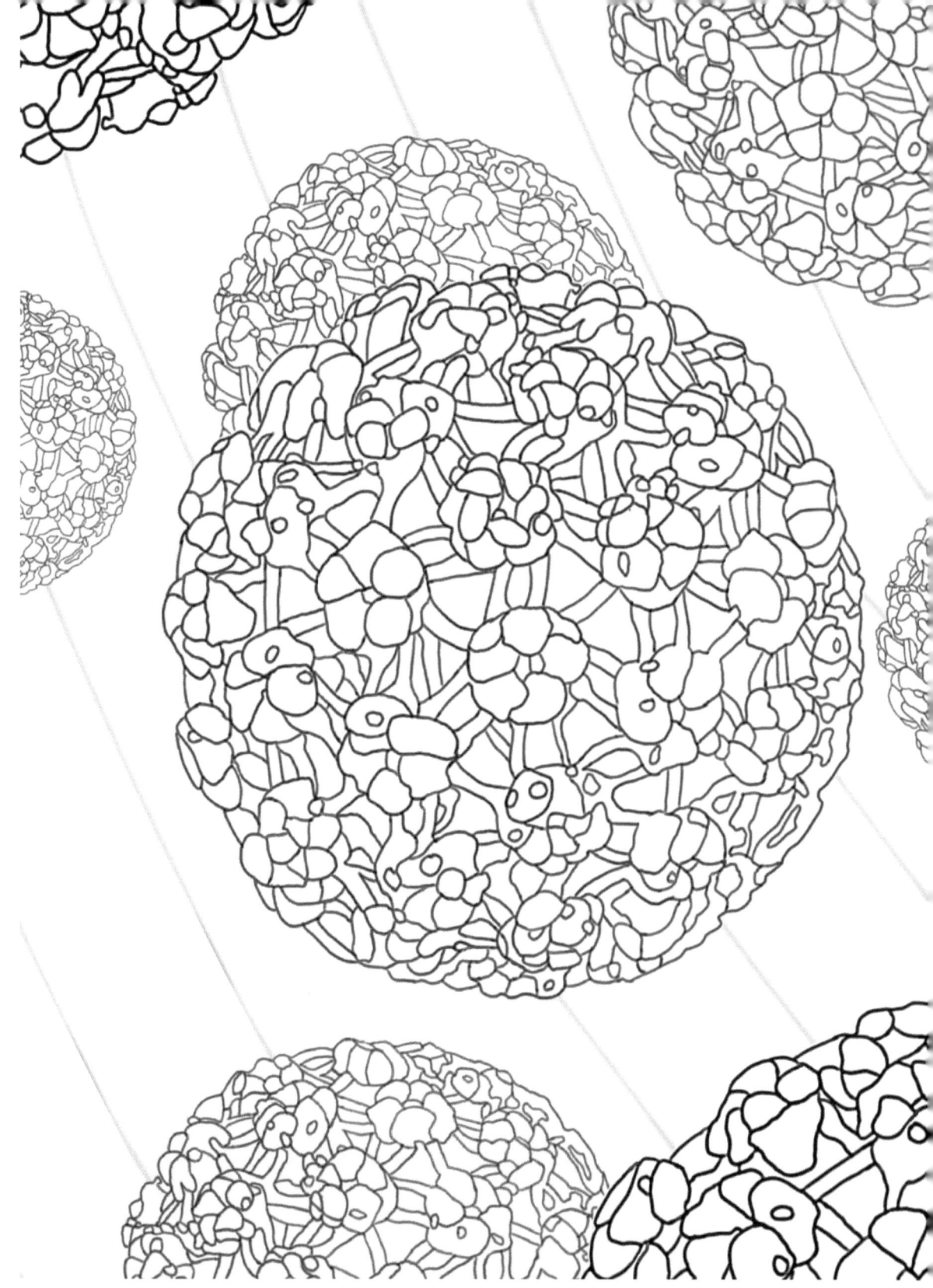

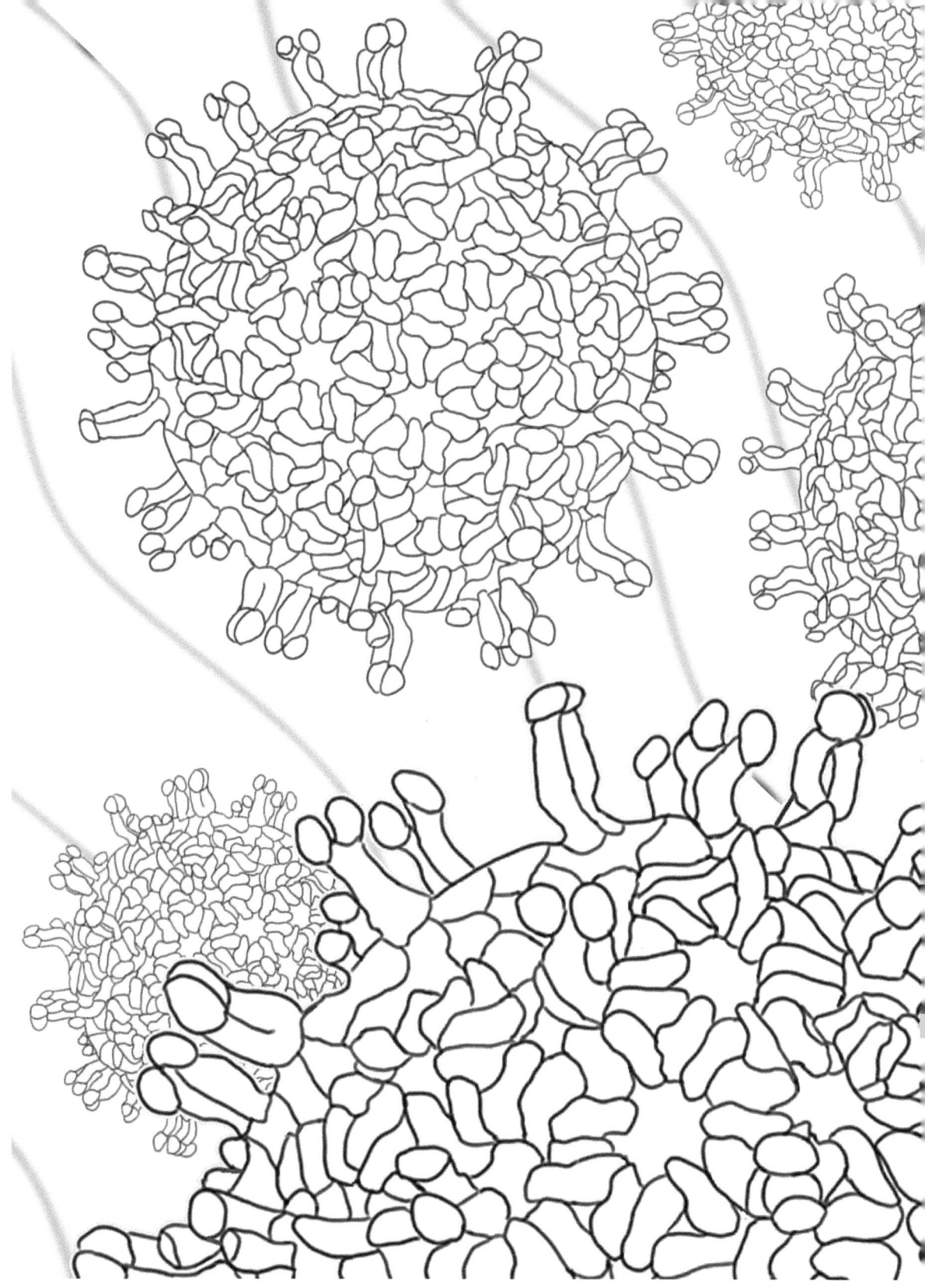

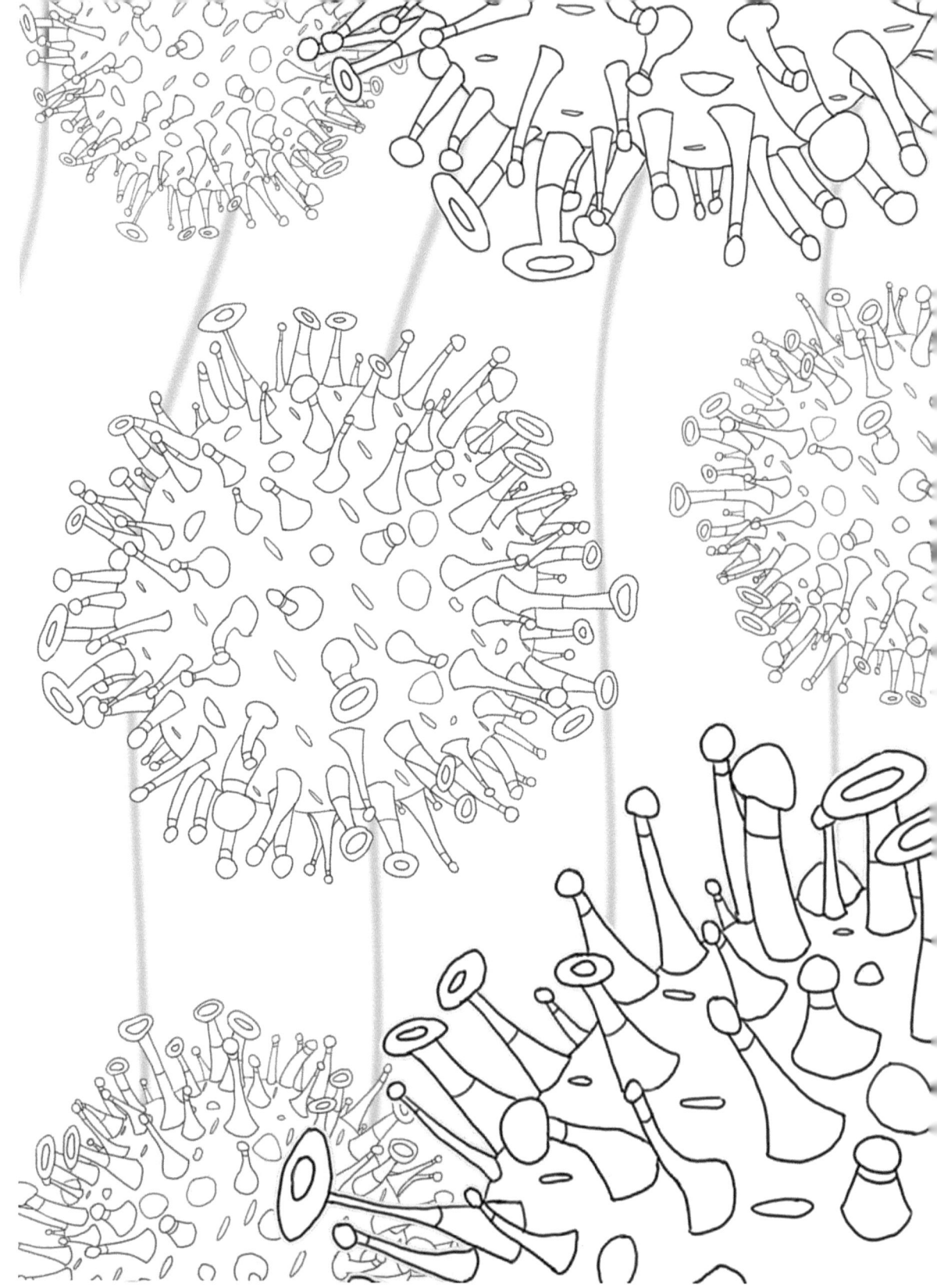

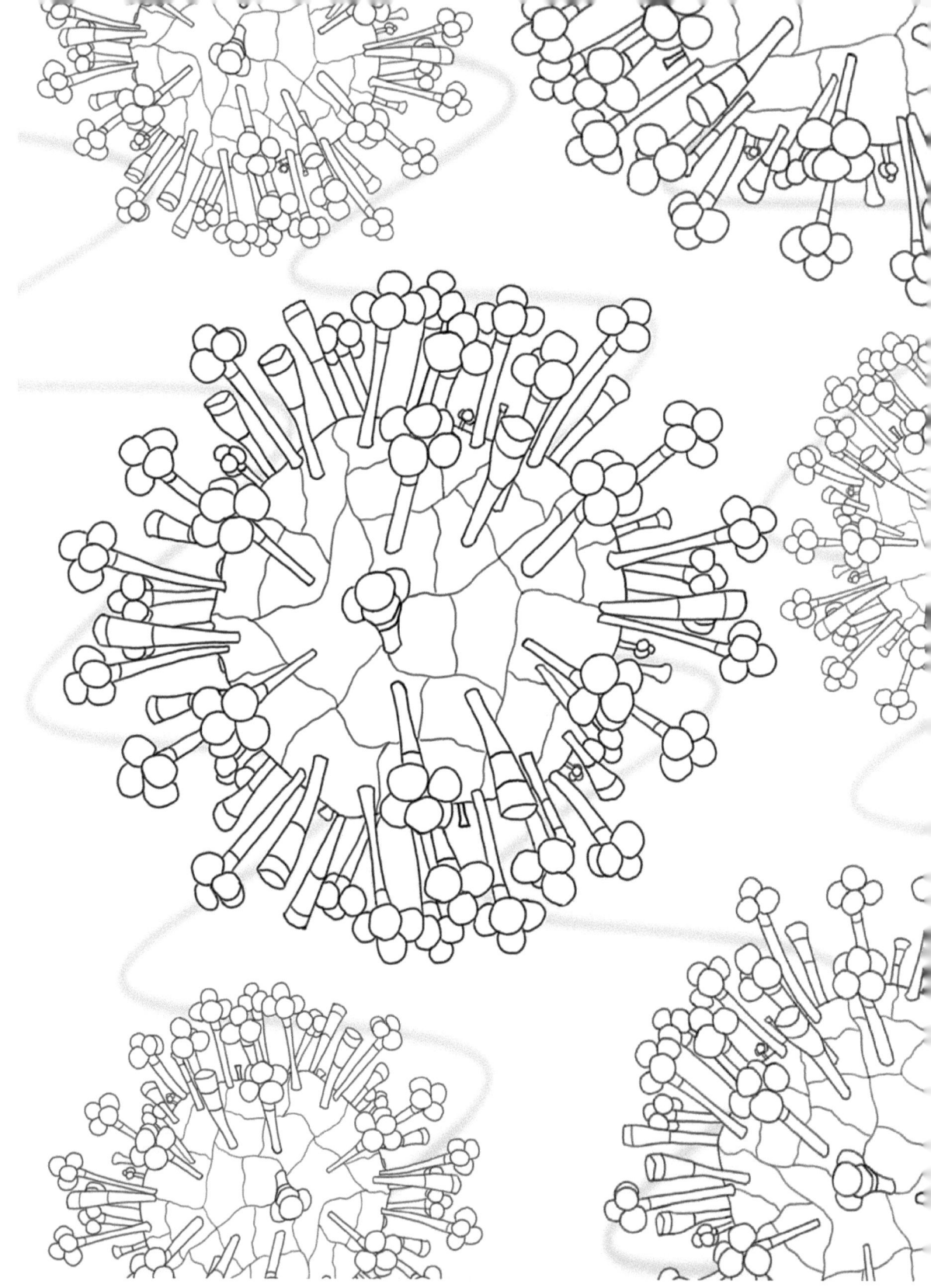

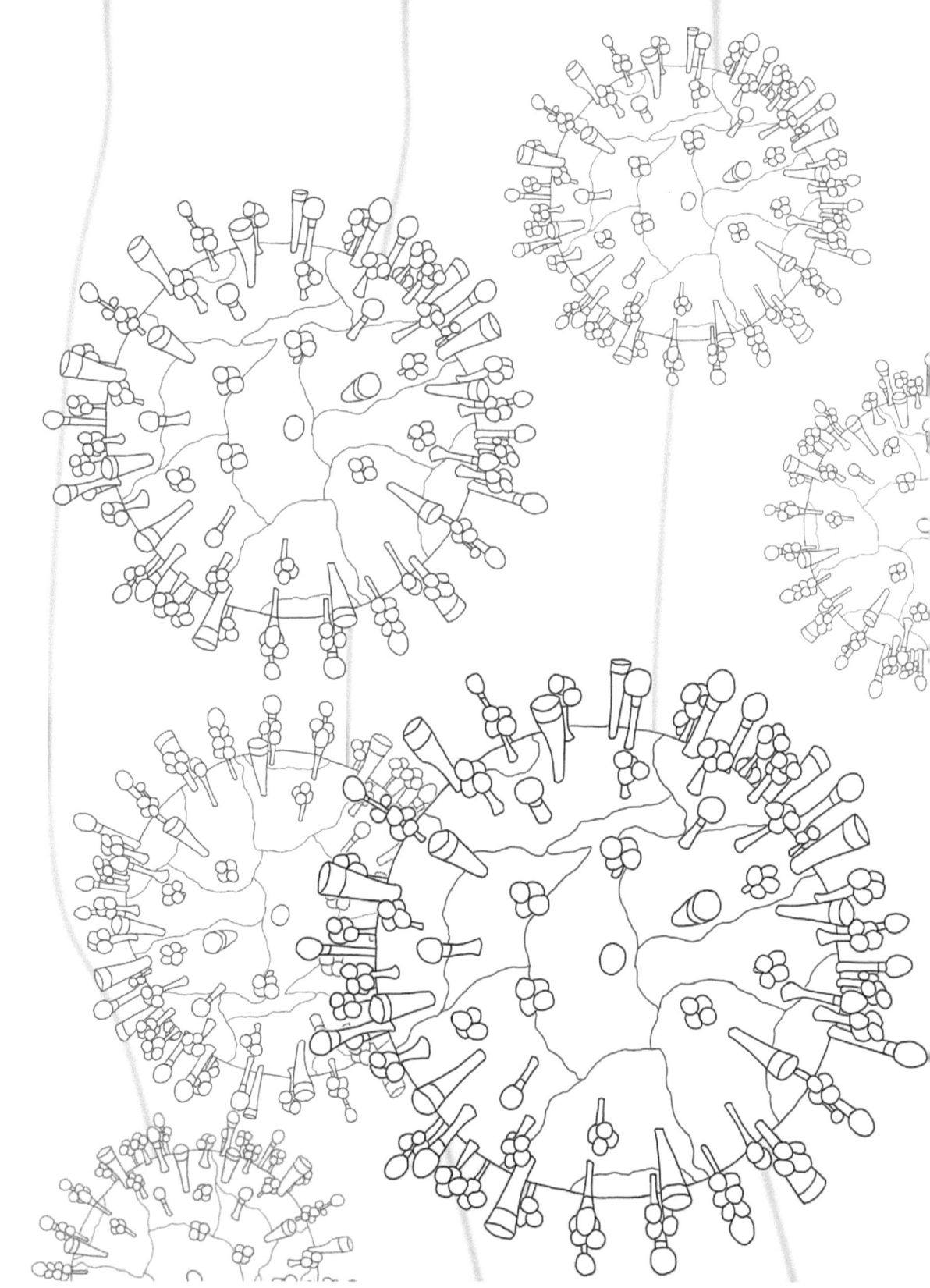

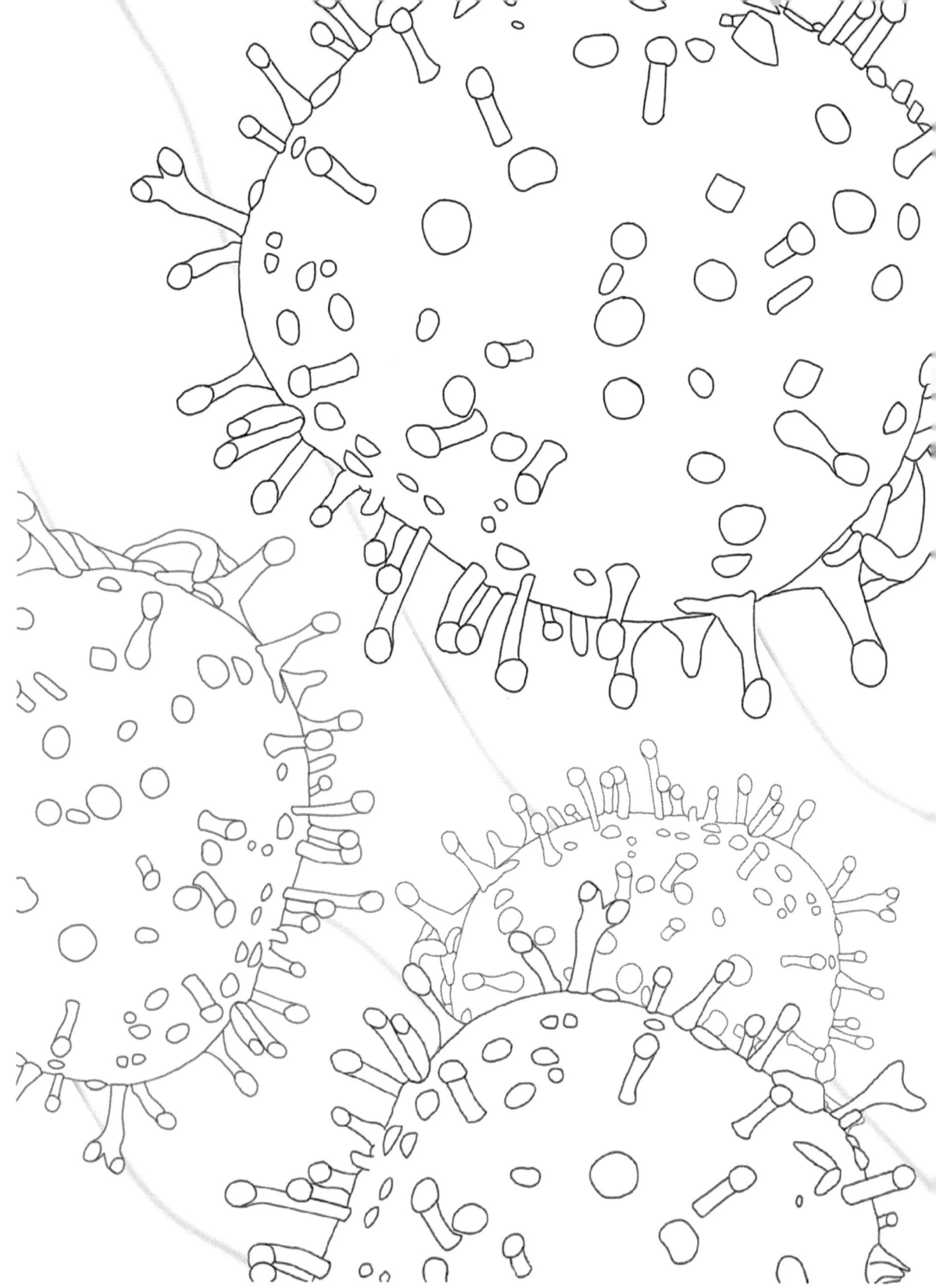

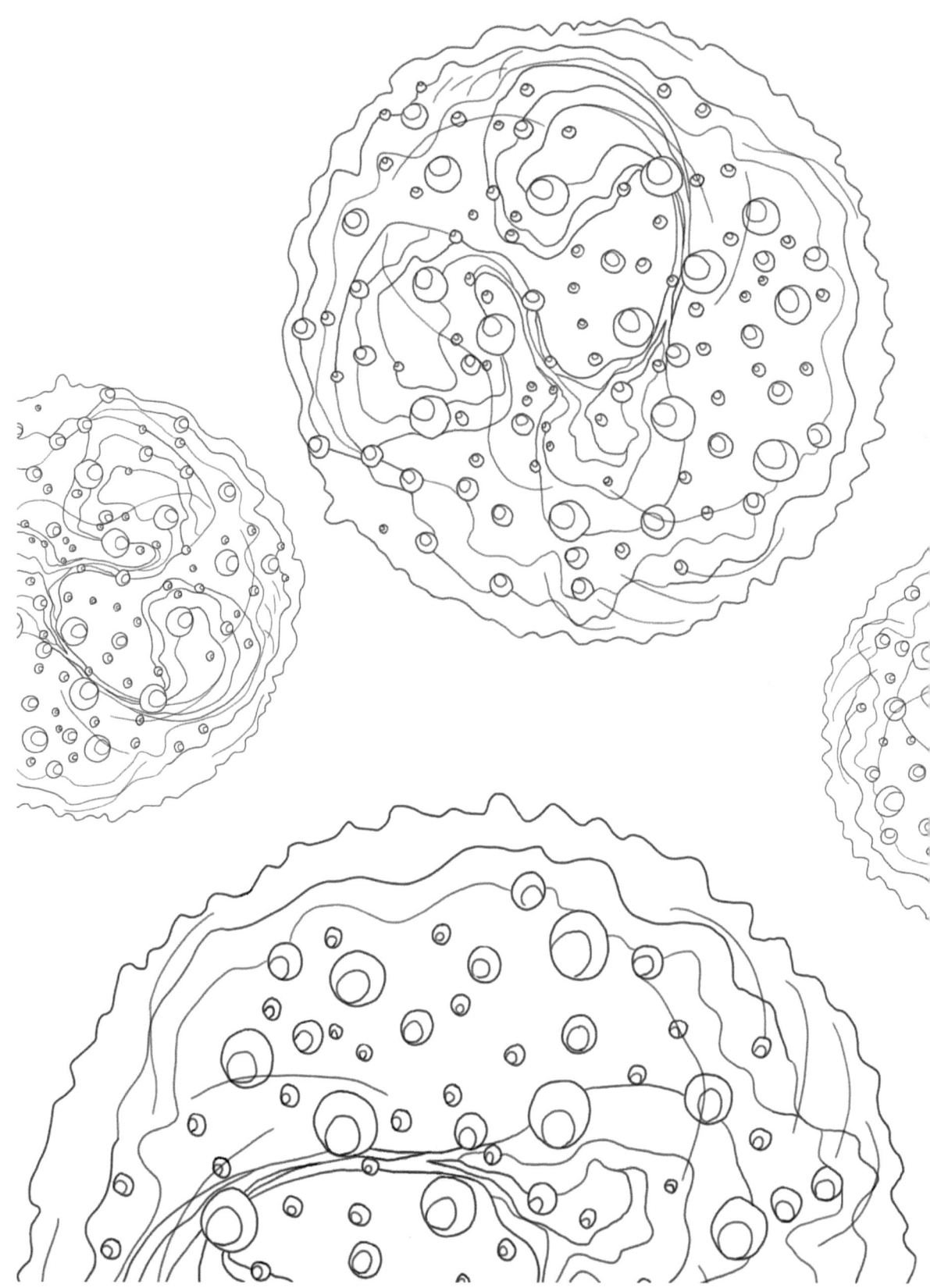

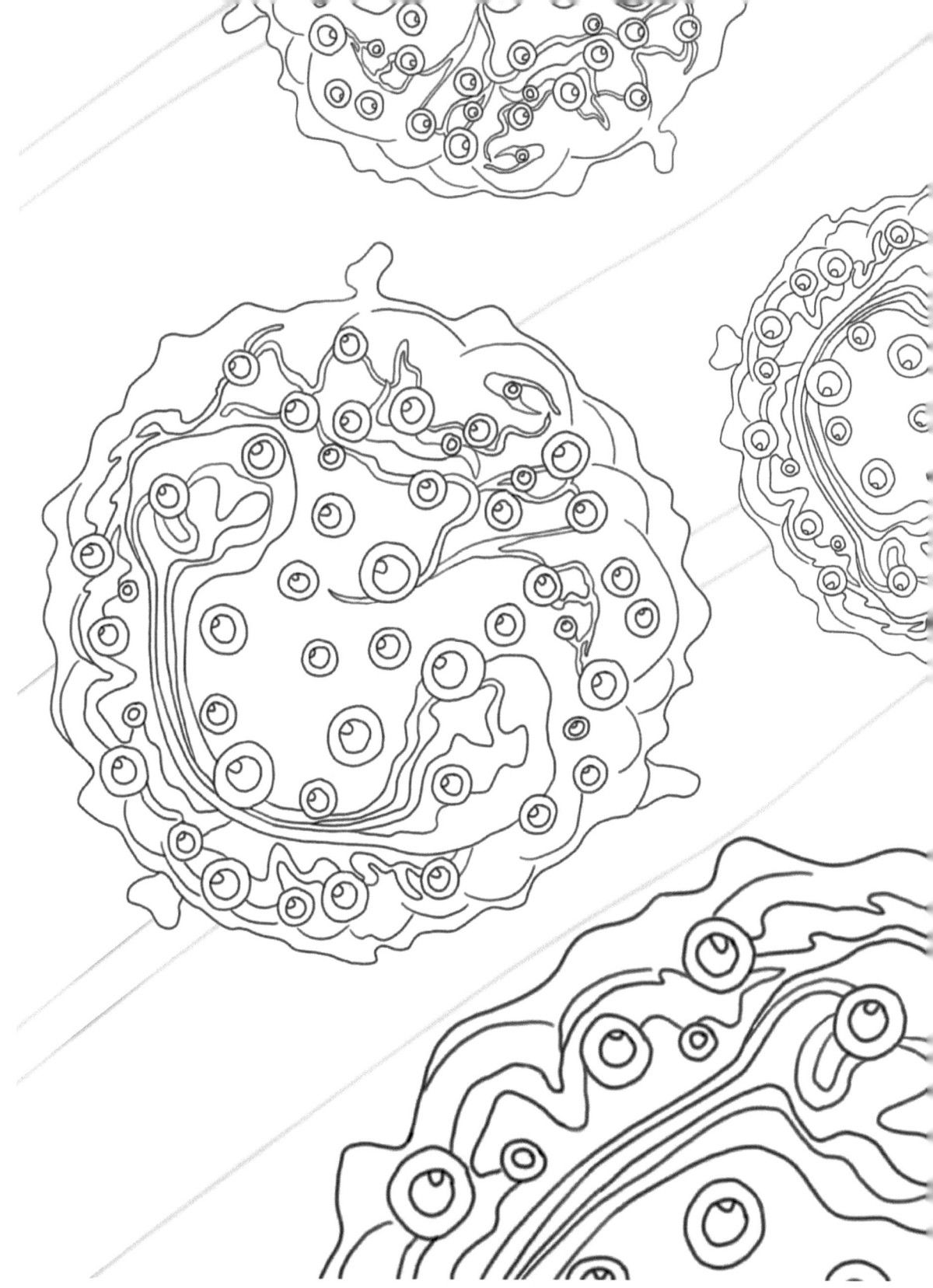

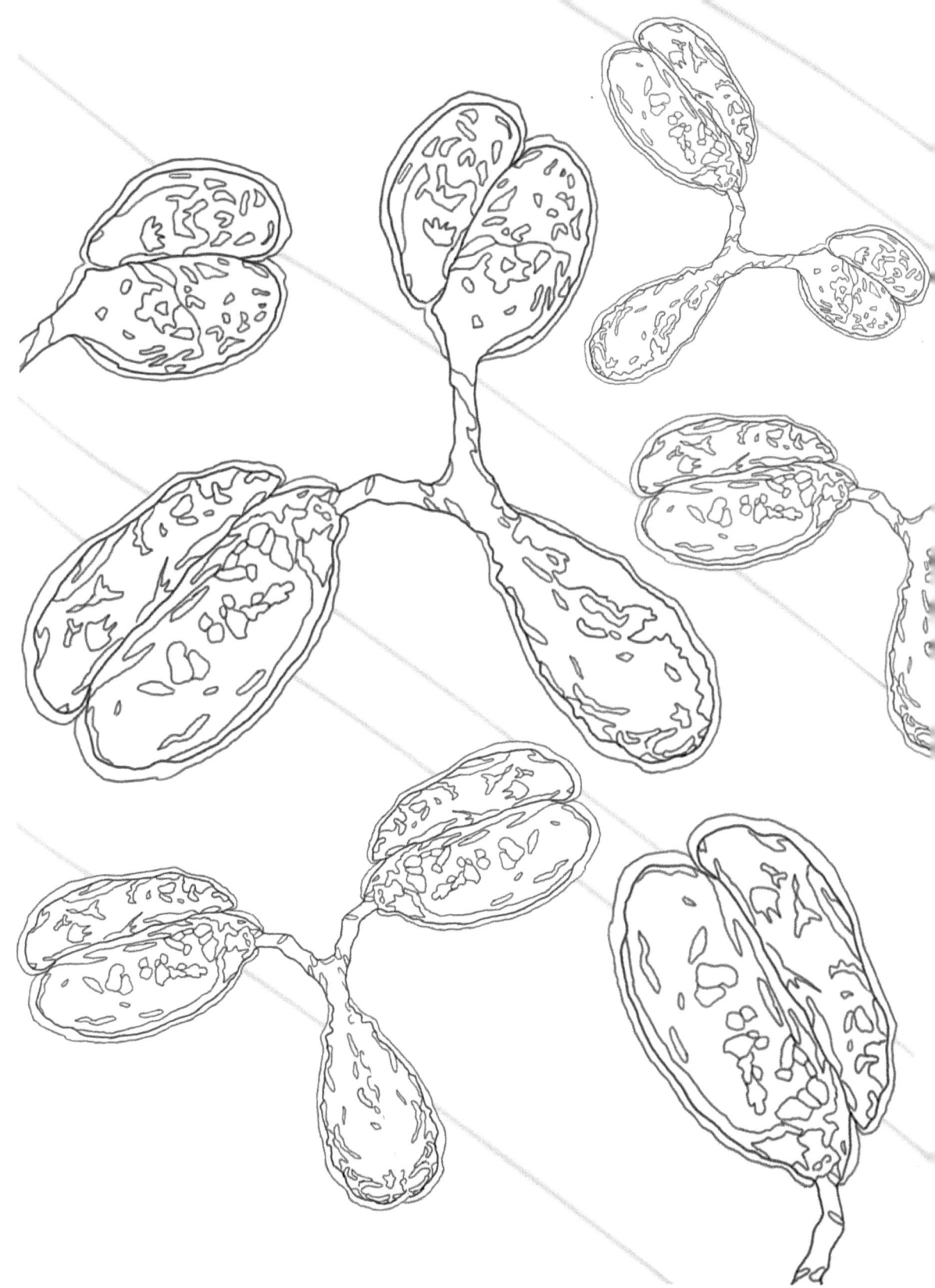

Further Books from Brian Gagg :

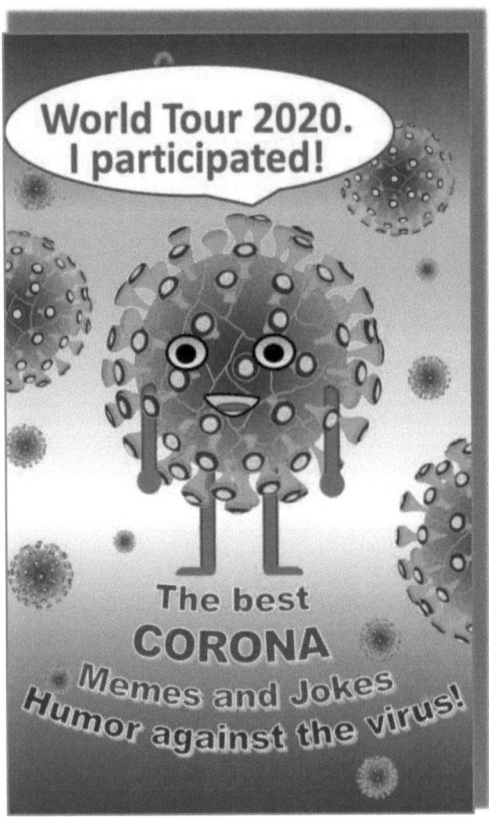

The best CORONA Memes and Jokes
Humor against the virus!

FCK CRN
Notebook